# Spiritual Spinach™

## Vol. I

## James Colaianni

*Spiritual Spinach, Vol. I*
by James Colaianni
Copyright 2001 James Colaianni

ISBN  1-58169-067-3
For Worldwide Distribution
Printed in the U.S.A.

Evergreen Press
P.O. Box 91011 • Mobile, AL 36691
800-367-8203
E-mail: info@evergreen777.com

# TABLE OF CONTENTS

## ACKNOWLEDGMENTS

With deepest appreciation, I wish to acknowledge the ongoing, reliable efforts of two very special co-workers—Sharon Walters and Todd Saunders.

To my indispensible, good-right-arm James Jr.—my thanks for his awe-inspiring, daily touches of genius cannot be adequately expressed in mere words.

To Rev. Eugene Zimmers—a very special thank you for your wisdom, encouragement, and support over the years.

Finally, to Patricia, my wife and the mother of our six children—thanks from the deepest level of my being for the touch of your hand and for your treasured editorial assistance.

# DEDICATION

*To Pat, Karen, Janice, James,*
*Louis and John, and in loving memory*
*of our beloved Pamela,*
*I dedicate this labor of love.*

# INTRODUCTION

Spiritual spinach! Change! The most important thing we can do for ourselves, both individually and as a people, is to embark on a plate-cleaning journey, deep down to the center of our beings, to the point of intimate encounter with the very Source of life. I am talking about that deep level where the soul is laid bare...where the real stock-taking occurs and the spinach is digested...where the cost of genuine human fulfillment is revealed as the most challenging thing of all: radical change.

At a high school commencement exercise in Washington, D.C., one of the senior girls delivered a closing prayer which she herself had written. The young woman began to read her prayer at a time when people began gathering their things to leave and their thoughts were turning to the parking lot. But, as the prayer unfolded, the noise quickly subsided and a miraculous silence settled over the crowd until the last word of the prayer was uttered. Here is a portion of that prayer:

> Dear God, grant us one thing before we leave the sheltered reassurance of our childhood. Show us life—not an empty, shallow world of shallow people

and shallow dreams, but real life. We want to change the world but we don't know how. We want to throw our arms around our brothers, but our hands cannot reach. We want to break the bonds of conformity that tie us to the ground, but we're not strong. Smile on us when we drink from the waters of truth. And, when we are old, reassure us that our struggle helped to make the world a world of peace, compassion and wisdom. And please don't let us die without ever having lived.

A genuinely thoughtful young woman getting to the heart of the matter. We want to throw our arms around our brothers and sisters. We want to be real. "Please, God, don't let us die without ever having lived." But we'll never know how to live this kind of life until we learn to eat our spiritual spinach. Eat! And change until the love of God is revealed to you as never before.

Many of the stories, anecdotes, real-life scenarios and mini-homilies are taken from my extensive collection of "Sunday Sermons," a periodical subscribed to by thousands of clergy in the U.S., Canada, Western Europe, Australia, and Africa. Some of the material was submitted over the years by loyal "Sunday

Sermons" subscribers. Many have been garnered from a variety of sources and, as far as possible, are presented with full attribution. Many others are residing comfortably in the public domain. And, of course, the well-known "Anonymous" is also represented.

—J.F.C.

In his heyday, the cartoon character, Popeye, was a sort of "Arnold Schwarzennager Without Guns." What the bad guys feared when Popeye confronted them were his muscles which propelled his fists. Whenever the need arose, Popeye would maximize his physical potential by downing a can of spinach, as he sang his song that told how strong spinach made him. Today, there is an ever-present need for us to maximize our spiritual potential—our life-enrichment potential—by downing daily doses of "spiritual spinach."

# PART ONE

# Spinach for Life

## THE NEED TO CHANGE

Psychiatrists tell us that a common complaint of their patients is "I don't seem to be going anywhere with my life"—reason enough, I suppose, to be in the grip of despair. One is reminded of the ancient parable of life in which a young sea horse said to his father...

"Give me my inheritance. It's time for me to live my own life. I'm going to seek my fortune." His father gave him ten gold coins, and the young sea horse eagerly swam away.

Before long, he met an eel who stopped him and asked, "Where are you going?"

He replied, "I'm going to seek my fortune!"

The eel said, "If you give me three of those gold coins, I'll let you have these electric

1

flippers that will get you there in half the time." The sea horse became excited. He gave the eel the coins and went on his way quicker than before.

After using his electric flippers for awhile, he met up with an octopus who asked, "Where are you going in such a hurry?"

"I'm going to seek my fortune!" exclaimed the sea horse.

"I'll sell you my aqua-scooter for three of your gold coins. Then you'll get to wherever you're going much faster." The sea horse, now more excited than ever, gave him the coins, hopped on the aqua-scooter and went on his way, faster than ever.

Soon he came upon a big shark who asked, "Where are you going?"

"I'm going to seek my fortune!" declared the sea horse in a rush.

"Well," said the shark, "if you'll give me those four coins I'll show you a shortcut that will get you there much quicker."

The sea horse was now beside himself with excitement. He gave the shark the last of his coins, adjusted his flippers, put his aqua-scooter into high gear and followed along the short-cut...right into the wide-open jaws of the shark. Unfortunately, the poor little sea horse was never to be heard from again.

Many people are like the little creature in the morality tale: they're in a big hurry, but have no clue as to where they're going, much less how to get there. They are in need of guidance and direction. In other words, they need to let God, not their "fortunes," be at the center of their lives. They will need to partake of some "spiritual spinach" in order to give them the strength to change.

# Genuine Life Goals

All the "self-help" books tell us that we need to have goals in life: financial, career, psychological, leisure-time, retirement, possessions, etc. In his own inimitable style, baseball's Yogi Berra once said, "You have to be very careful if you don't know where you're going because you might not get there." Despite his unique way of phrasing it, we all know what Yogi means. We all need to have goals, but if we don't establish our life goals within the context of God's plan for our ultimate destination, we might never get there. When we are pursuing genuine life-goals, we discover that the happiest people in the world are those who tailor their lives to God's purpose.

# FULL SPEED AHEAD TO NOWHERE

We eat, we work, we shop, we run around, and we get tired. We get physically weary. We get emotionally weary. We get spiritually weary. And we wonder why our lives seem to be going full speed ahead to nowhere—aimlessly, pointlessly, recklessly.

I got up early one morning,
And rushed right into the day;
I had so much to accomplish,
I didn't have time to pray.

Troubles just tumbled about me,
And heavier came each task.
*Why doesn't God help me?* I wondered,
He answered, "You didn't ask."

I wanted to see joy and beauty,
But the day toiled on grey and bleak.
I called on the Lord for the reason.
He said, "You didn't seek."

The anonymous poet then wrote a little epilogue:

I woke up early one morning,
and paused before entering the day.
I had so much to accomplish,
That I had to take time to pray.

"I *had to take time* to pray." The spiritual pause that refreshes is absolutely necessary for our life-enrichment. There is no way to maintain spiritual good health without prayer—without stopping to listen to the inner-voice of the Spirit of God deep within your soul.

The great scientist, Isaac Newton, was a man rooted in prayer, which is to say, rooted in God. He once said:

"I can take my telescope and look millions and millions of miles into space. But I can lay it aside and go into my room, shut the door, get down on my knees and see more of heaven and get closer to God than I can assisted by all the telescopes and material things on earth."

# Heavy Burden It Is

The "Fable of the Birds" is a story about creation. All the newly made animals were walking around discovering what it was like to be alive—all, that is, except the birds! They stood around complaining because God had given them a heavy burden that he'd given no other animal—awkward appendages attached to their shoulders.

They thought that God must be punishing them somehow. They couldn't figure out why they had to carry them around, making it hard to walk. "Why?" they asked. "What good are these things?" Finally, three of the more adventurous birds began to move their appendages up and down. They began to flutter them quicker and quicker, and they discovered that the very thing they had regarded as a burden actually made it possible for them to fly! Soon all the birds were soaring up into the sky. The "heavy burden" they were carrying around turned out to be a beautiful gift.

Many of us act like those silly birds. We regard God's call to obedience as an awkward appendage to our lives—weighing us down. *Thou shalt not...! Thou shalt...!* Heavy burden it is until we discover that God's law is really the sacred wind that enables us to fly.

# TOUCHED BY GOD'S GLORY

This is a little nature story in which the author shares his insight with us:

"We were hiking in the mountains out West when I saw the stone, a small one, about the size of a half-dollar, with smooth rounded edges. Ordinarily I would have passed it by, not being a rock hound. It would have remained there for another thousand years perhaps, a mere pebble among the larger stones on the trail. But this one instantly caught my eye. It was special. Glinting in the sunlight, it seemed to reflect all the surrounding colors, as though trying to mirror nature. Into my pocket went the rare find.

"All the way home to the East Coast I though about where I should display it so its beauty could be most enjoyed. I finally placed it in a curio cabinet, next to some jade and carved ivory. I forgot about it for a while. Then one day, while dusting, I was surprised to see that the stone had completely lost its luster. It sat on the shelf among the other lovely objects, a hard, gray chunk of nothing, downright ugly. I was shocked. What had happened to the prize I had so carefully brought back with me across the continent? Where was the sparkle and the colors that had attracted me so much?

"Disgusted, I snatched it up and started for the kitchen door to throw it out. Then, just as I opened it, a beam of light struck the stone. As though by magic, it began to shimmer and glow again. In an instant, the beautiful jewel tones shone brilliantly. Had they returned? Or had they always been there, dormant, waiting to be released? Wondering, I glanced up at the sky. Sunlight! That was the answer. The rays from the sun were all my stone needed to come alive."

How much like each of us! Of ourselves our lives are empty, colorless, without meaning. Only when we are touched by the glory of God is our inner beauty revealed.

# Time to Resign

A man we shall call "George" was successful in business. He had a devoted wife and three lovely children. He had a comfortable house in the suburbs, complete with swimming pool. By certain standards, George "had it made."

One day he began to experience restlessness within himself about his life. Tensions mounted as he tried to cope with the pressures of his business and of life in today's world. Finally, he had a breakdown of sorts, which brought him to realize that he had to do some things to change his life situation. Among other things, he started going to church again, after an absence of many years. Gradually, he came to understand the nature and meaning of Christ's presence in a whole new way.

Later, in one revealing sentence, George summarized what he had done to enrich his life. He said, "I submitted my resignation as 'Chief-Executive-of-the-Universe' and God accepted it."

# LET GOD!

There was a wise old pastor who was well-known for his skill in counseling. Not only was he a good listener but also a good advisor. He had that rare gift of analysis which enabled him to cut through all the verbal trappings, get to the heart of the problem, and deal with it. He willingly and lavishly gave of his time to all those who came to him with their problems. But frequently, after much listening, careful questioning, and serious reflection, he found no real core problem to deal with.

One day he counseled an uptight man who was worried sick about what might have been and what might come to pass "if only I had done this" and "if only I could do that."

In the view of this wise pastor, the best advice he had to offer the man was simply to say, "Let go and let God." That is to say, "You have reached that point where you must surrender both the unrecoverable past and the unpredictable future to Divine Providence. Break free from the enslaving notion that you have it within your power to wish away past events or to control the unfolding of future events. "Let go and let God!" He does indeed have "the whole world in His hands."

# It Came To Pass!

Religious Philosopher Eric Butterworth once was confronted with an extremely difficult life situation. He felt as if he had a tremendous weight on his shoulders. He began looking everywhere for help, asking everyone he knew for insight, trying somehow to get a thought that would lead him to a solution to his problem.

Finally, he began leafing through the pages of the Bible, and his finger came to rest on the words, "It came to pass." Although these words appear over and over in the Scriptures, nevertheless, in themselves, they are almost meaningless. But Eric Butterworth kept looking at them.

Suddenly, in his words, "A light dawned. This experience that I'm having didn't come to stay! It came to pass! I began to realize that the problem hadn't come to burden me, it had come to bring me something that I needed for my growth."

# VALLEY OF LOVE AND DELIGHT

In a popular recording of the forties, Bing Crosby sang, "Give Me the Simple Life." That's good theology. It might well have been inspired by an old New England "Shaker" hymn:

It is a gift to be simple.
It is a gift to be free.
It is a gift to come down
    to where we ought to be.
And when we find ourselves
    to be in the place just right,
It will be in the Valley of Love and
    Delight.

Those New England Shakers embraced their simple way of life as a great gift. The "Valley of Love and Delight" was, for them, simply to spend time with God.

# A CRIPPLING DISEASE

According to one of author Ernest Hemingway's biographers, on the first day of each new year Hemingway gave away some of his most treasured possessions. When people asked him why he did this, he would answer, "If I can give them away, then I own them. But if I can't give them away, they own me."

Psychiatrists and clinical psychologists have been telling us for a long time that it is the economic aspect of their lives that troubled patients are most reluctant to reveal. They are willing to bare their souls about their work, their home, their sex-life, their leisure-life, but not their finances. This, it seems, is the last secret to unfold, the most painful to reveal. Why is that so?

Is it because of the popular, but misguided belief that money empowers us to move into some kind of guaranteed future of our own making? Is it because we have been victimized by the terribly mistaken notion that genuine human fulfillment is measured in terms of the amount of money and things we have acquired? One prominent psychiatrist has described love of money as the most crippling disease in the Western world.

Despite one man's tremendous success in

the world of business and finance, he became extremely depressed. A terrible feeling of emptiness had come over him. He searched in many directions, but nothing seemed to help. Finally, a psychiatrist referred the troubled man to a member of the clergy. Perhaps a spiritual checkup would help.

After listening to the man's tale of woe, the spiritual advisor opened up a Bible and proceeded to mark off certain sections for the man to read. "After you have gone over this material, I want you to come back to see me," he said.

Several days later, the man returned and said, "I've followed your instructions. I've read all the material you marked off. In fact, I've gone through it several times." To which the spiritual counselor replied, "Now the question is, Has it gone through you?"

Have you eaten your spiritual spinach today?

# Isn't It Amazing?

At the conclusion of a week-long prayer and meditation retreat, the participants were asked to write down their impressions. One man wrote:

"My ambition to succeed had taken over my life to such an extent that I was feeling out of touch with reality; I was missing out on life. So I came here looking for an answer. I came here looking for some sign or miracle. And what I've discovered is that the real miracle is the miracle of the people: the way they greet one another and open up their hearts to each other. Here everything is so simple and basic you can read the signs that are written everywhere in life. When you're moving too fast, you can't read the signs. When you're moving too fast you miss the miracle of life."

You begin to get your best possible glimpse of the miracle of life when you realize that you are special in God's creative plan. You are one of God's "originals"—wonderfully unique. Like the universe itself, your life is constantly in motion. You are necessary! You belong! God's plan for the fulfillment of His creation includes you. He needs *you!*

Do you really appreciate the miracle of who you are? Do you appreciate the wonder of your body, for instance? Amazing are your ears that know both sound and silence. Amazing is your bone structure, the clean lines of your arms and legs, the dexterity of your hands. Amazing is the flow of your blood through its vessels. Amazing is the journey of a thought through the mazes of your brain. Amazing is the breath that fans the fires of your life. Amazing is the way food is transformed into living cells. Amazing is the way life begets life, and another living soul comes into being. Isn't it amazing?

Do you appreciate the miracle of your mind? With your mind you can create beauty, search for truth, dream noble dreams. With your mind you can explore the present, recall the past, plan the future. With your mind you can gain dominion over the earth, achieve mastery of yourself, fly toward God. Isn't it amazing?

Do you appreciate the miracle of your own spirit? You are one with the living God...the God who fashioned the physical universe, the simplest secrets of which our wisest physicists are only now discovering. You are one with the God who, in a living cell, effortlessly creates substance that all our chemists in acres of factories cannot duplicate. You are one with the God who fashioned the human soul and made it so wonderful and strange that even you who possess it cannot see its full meaning. As the leaves are a part of the tree, as the sands are a part of the earth, as the cells of your body are part of you, so you are part of the spirit of God. Isn't it amazing![1]

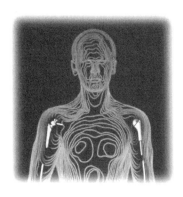

# GOD'S MASTERPIECES

From our school-days we remember the traditional "Seven Wonders" of the ancient world: The Pyramids of Egypt, the Hanging Gardens of Babylon, the Lighthouse of Alexandria, and so on. The *Sunday Times Magazine* of London once asked several well-known persons to choose the seven wonders of the modern world.

The results evoked much debate. Lord Kenneth Clark, for example, selected the "Concorde" aircraft as one of his choices. A famous photographer included American hamburgers on his list. Novelist Anthony Burgess put champagne high on his list. Another novelist mentioned Disneyland. Other selections included the aurora borealis (or northern lights), the Great Wall of China, New York City, the city of Venice, and the Taj Mahal.

Like the original list, this modern list did not include God's own first choice. In God's eyes, we are the "Wonders of the World." We humans are the masterpieces of His creation.

# Partnership with God

Several years ago, a man died leaving his wife with six children to raise. The widow reflected seriously on her talents and what she would do with the rest of her life. She realized that she loved children and had a way with them. Consequently, she decided to take in several foster children—in addition to her own six. For years she ran a beautiful, loving home for all those children. From time to time, she needed help and received it largely from people in her church community. As the years went by, the children turned out beautifully. A newspaper reporter came to interview her for a feature story.

The reporter asked, "How in the world have you managed to raise so many children so gracefully?"

The woman replied with a smile, "Well, it was the partnership."

"What partnership?" asked the reporter.

Still smiling, the woman answered, "My partnership with God. A few days after my husband died, I looked at my situation and I said to God, 'From now on, Lord, I'll do the work if you'll do the worrying!' And all through the years I've done what needed to be done. I have upheld my end of the bargain."

Then her smile broadened, and she said with great joy in her voice, "And He upheld His!"

Even when it seems as though the total anxieties of the whole world will come crashing down on you, trust in your deliverance by a gracious God who will never abandon you. Uphold your end of the bargain. God will uphold His.

---

It was September, 1715 when the funeral of Louis XIV was held in Paris. Louis XIV: the man who had said, "I am the State"; the man who built Versailles; the man who was called the "Sun King" because of the lavishness of his Court. Who was a more powerful king than Louis XIV? At his funeral service, the Bishop of Paris was to preach the eulogy. Thousands of people had come, spilling out of the Cathedral into the square beyond. The bishop went up into the pulpit and preached a eulogy consisting of just four words. Then he left the pulpit and continued the service. The four words he had preached were: Only God is great!

# YOU ARE UNIQUE

In the famous story by Antoine de Saint-Exupery, "The Little Prince" had one possession he considered unique in all the universe. His rose was the most beautiful living thing he could ever imagine, and he had raised her and joyously cared for her. By day he would gently water her and tend the soil around her delicate stem, and at night he would cover her with a glass globe to protect her from any harm. Her soft laughter filled him with the most amazing feelings of fulfillment, and her singular beauty made his small planet complete.

When the Little Prince came to visit Earth, one of the first sights he happened upon was a whole garden filled with roses, all laughing and chatting and filling the air with their familiar perfume. The Little Prince stared at them, overcome with the realization that his rose was only one of numberless others that flourished in the universe.

He laid down on the ground and wept. But, slowly, as he listened to the happy sounds flowing out of the garden, a deeper thought came to him, and a feeling of contentment began to stir. His rose was unique. She was the object of *his* unique love—different from all other roses.

Everyone who has ever been loved is unique in this sense. It begins with God's unique love for each individual human being. God loves each of us in a way that is special to us because we are different from every other person. And when we love another person, we do so in a way that is special to that person for the same reason.

Consider the man who received a Ph.D. from Oxford University. The thesis for his degree was entitled: "The Influence of the Motion of Fish Tails Upon the Tides of the Ocean." That's right! And he proved, to his satisfaction a least, that the great tides of the world are influenced by the motion of even the smallest of fish tails. You who think your life is purposeless and doesn't count for anything—do you think for one moment that the God who created such a Universe in which every movement has meaning can overlook you?

# THANK GOD!

According to an ancient fable, there once lived in a small village a man whose body was so twisted and whose face was so disfigured that the townspeople laughed at him...the children teased him...and the dogs barked at him. The man became so embittered that he left the village and went deep into the forest, where he lived alone. There he found a measure of solace in the beauty of each sunrise and sunset, in the soft sighing of the breeze in the trees, in the frolic of the creatures of the forest, and in the sweet songs of the birds of the air. Still the bitterness only softened. It did not go away.

One day, a visitor came into the hermit's hut. As they sat down together to an evening meal, the hermit asked the visitor to offer a prayer.

The visitor replied, "No, you are the master here. It is you who must say the blessing."

And so the hermit, nervous at first, spoke his gratitude for the beauty of the forest and the wonder of nature and the nourishment they were about to share.

Whereupon the visitor said: "You have forgotten one thing. You have neglected to thank

24

God for yourself." The hermit looked away, saying nothing. The visitor continued: "You have retreated into the forest because you have despaired of your physical unattractiveness. You have forgotten that in the eyes of God, you are far more beautiful than all the trees and all the flowers and all the birds of the forest."

The hermit could not forget those words, and when the opportunity came, he moved back to the town of his birth. Strange as it may seem, the people of the community no longer laughed when he walked by. The children no longer teased him. His heart sang with joy for he realized that he was living in the same town, with the same people, but now everything was different! It was different because he was different. He had learned to thank God for himself.[2]

# PART TWO

# Spinach to Serve Others

## LEARNING LOVE

Pop singer Cliff Richard visited a Bihari refugee camp in Bangledesh. When he returned home, he described a moving incident:

"The first morning I was there I must have washed my hands a dozen times. I didn't want to touch anything, least of all the people. Everyone in those camps was covered in sores and scabs.

"I was bending down to one little mite, mainly for the photographer's benefit, and trying hard not to come too close. Just then, someone accidentally stood on the child's finger. He screamed and, as a reflex, I grabbed him, forgetting his dirt and his sores. I remember that warm little body clinging to me and his crying instantly stopping. In that moment I knew I had much to learn about practical loving, but that at least I'd started."[3]

# THE ULTIMATE MIRACLES

In the play called "Harvey," the main character is a man named Elwood P. Dodd—an eccentric, friendly man whose closest friend is an enormous, invisible rabbit named Harvey. When he first met Harvey, he saw the giant leaning against a lamppost at the corner of 18th and Fairfax Streets.

His family, however, is incensed at the embarrassment that Elwood is causing them, and they soon hire Dr. Chumley, a psychiatrist. But a funny thing happens as Dr. Chumley tries to "cure" Elwood and rid his family of Harvey's embarrassing presence. The psychiatrist experiences a spectacular turn around in his own life.

In one scene he says, "Flyspecks. I've been spending my life among flyspecks while miracles have been leaning on lampposts at 18th and Fairfax." Later, after talking further with Elwood, the doctor tosses aside his pad and pencil and joyfully declares, "I've got to have that rabbit!"

The rabbit, of course, is a metaphor for a miracle. Many of us are like Dr. Chumley, living among flyspecks when there may be miracles leaning against lampposts on our own street corners. And the miracles are much better than giant, invisible rabbits. They are golden sunsets and flowering gardens, majestic oceans and colorful rainbows. But most of all, they are people. They are people of all shapes and sizes and personalities and customs and colors. They may look or act different by our ordinary standards, but they have something to contribute, something to tell us, something to teach us because they are more sensitive than we are to the miracles all around us.

Like Dr. Chumley, we need to open our minds and hearts to the miracle of life and joyously exclaim, "I've got to have those people"—and laugh with them and cry with them and be amazed by them! Because it is in people that a living, loving God is everywhere to be found and experienced—through the miracle of love.

Frances Bacon once said, "It is not what we eat but what we digest that makes us strong; not what we gain but what we save that makes us rich; not what we read but what we remember that makes us learned; not what we preach but what we practice that makes us whole."

# A PERSON'S HEART

There is a wonderful passage in "Zorba the Greek" in which Zorba says:

"One day when I was a child, an old man took me on his knee and placed his hand on my head as though he were giving me his blessing. He said, 'I'm going to tell you a secret. You're too small to understand now, but you'll understand when you are bigger. Listen, little one: neither the seven stories of heaven nor the seven stories of the earth are enough to contain God.'"

It's already a great lesson on the vastness of divinity. But listen as the old man gets to the best part:

"Neither the seven stories of heaven nor the seven stories of the earth are enough to contain God, but a person's heart can contain God. So be very careful—and may my blessing go with you—never to wound another person's heart."

# WORTH LISTENING TO

The famous longshoreman/philosopher/ author, Eric Hofer, was cared for as a child by a Bavarian peasant woman after his mother had died. During this period of his life, Eric Hofer was blind. Years later, he had this to say about the woman who cared for him:

"This woman, Martha was her name, took loving care of me. I remember she was a big woman, and she must have really loved me because I remember those eight years of blindness in my childhood as essentially a happy time of my life. I remember a lot of talk and a lot of laughter. I must have talked a great deal as a child because Martha used to say to me again and again, "Do you remember when you said this? Do you remember when you said that?" And I remembered what I had said. All my life I have had a feeling about myself that what I think and what I say are worth listening to and remembering. This is the gift she gave me!"

When we give others the feeling that what they think and what they say are worth listening to, we are offering them one of the priceless gifts of love.

# LOVE THY NEIGHBOR

In her autobiography, *My Life in Three Acts,* the renowned actress, Helen Hayes, tells the moving story of how the transforming power of God affected her life in a time of deep distress:

"When my daughter died of polio, everybody stretched out a hand to help me, but at first, I couldn't seem to bear the touch of anything, even the love of friends; no support seemed strong enough.

"While Mary was still sick, I used to go early in the morning to a little church near the hospital to pray. There the working people came quietly to worship. I had been careless with my religion, I had rather cut God out of my life, and I didn't have the nerve at the time to ask Him to make my daughter well. I only asked Him to help me understand, to let me come in and reach Him. I prayed there every morning, and I kept looking for a revelation, but nothing happened.

"And then, much later, I discovered that it had happened, right there in the church. I could recall, vividly, one by one, the people I had seen there—the solemn laborers with tired looks, the old women with gnarled hands. Life had knocked them around, but for a brief moment they were being refreshed by an ennobling experience. It seemed, as they prayed, their worn faces lighted up, and they became the vessels of God. Here was my revelation. Suddenly I realized I was one of them. In my need I gained strength from the knowledge that they too had needs, and I felt an interdependence with them. I experienced a flood of compassion for people. I was learning the meaning of 'Love thy neighbor.'"[4]

The social activist Julia Ward Howe once asked Senator Charles Sumner to use his influence to intercede for a constituent who desperately needed help. The Senator responded, "Julia, these days I've become so busy and involved in so many matters of importance to the nation that I no longer have time to direct my attention to the concerns of individuals." Julia replied, "Senator, that is quite remarkable! Even God hasn't reached that stage yet!"

# THE FORCE WITHIN

Syndicated newspaper columnist Sidney J. Harris tells the story of visiting a certain friend who was a Quaker. Each night the friend would go to the same newsstand to buy a paper, and he always had a cheerful greeting for the newsdealer. He would say, "Nice to see you. You're looking good, how's business?" But the newsdealer's response was always curt, even sarcastic.

After observing these encounters for several nights, Sydney Harris said to his Quaker friend, "You are always so kind to that fellow. How can you be so friendly toward him when he is so nasty to you?"

To which the Quaker replied, "Why should I let him decide how I am going to act?"

For many of us, that is an important key to understanding one of the changes we need to make in our lives. Many of us unconsciously allow others to decide how we are going to act. We justify responding to hostility with hostility, saying, "Of course, I'm upset. You'd be upset too if you had this so-and-so to deal with." But that only reveals that our lives are being controlled by outside forces rather than the spiritually nourishing Force within.

# Strengthen Your Roots!

The 20th century: an incredible era of modern technology! Rockets blasted off to distant space targets, often landing with pinpoint accuracy. Thousands of people shuttled daily from continent to continent by mammoth jetliners. Robots with movable arms built automobiles on computerized assembly lines that moved more swiftly and precisely than those formerly run by humans.

The 20th century was also an incredible era of artificial beauty. Men with polished, handsome features and women with radiant, unblemished skin (both aided by an artist's airbrush) looked out from billboards and magazine covers, challenging one and all to follow them into the fantasy world of the macho-man and the glamorous woman.

Technology and glamour. Men and women, young and old are still searching for happiness that seems always just out of reach. They are still victims of a culture that promises satisfaction, but satisfaction cannot deliver them. They are prey to a culture that excites the senses but cannot nourish the soul.

Once upon a time, there was a tree. The tree was stately, but it knew that its massive strength was beginning to wane. When the wind was strong it felt itself shaking ominously and heard suspicious creaks in its limbs. So, with much effort, it grew another branch and then it felt stronger and safer than ever. But when the next gale blew, there was a terrific snapping of roots and, had it not been for the support of a friendly neighboring tree, it would have fallen flat to the ground.

When it had recovered from the shock, the tree looked at its neighbor curiously and asked, "Tell me, how is it that you not only have stood your ground, but are able to help me also?"

"Oh," replied the friend, "I'd be glad to tell you. When you were so busy growing your new branches, I was busy strengthening my roots."

# THE GRACIOUS CIRCLE

A woman lost her husband and went into an extended period of grief. She took flowers to the cemetery weekly but secluded herself from all other activities. Her doctor became concerned about her health when symptoms of physical illness began to appear. One day, he told her about two of his patients in a nearby hospital who had no families to visit them.

The doctor said to the grieving woman, "Next Sunday, instead of taking flowers to the cemetery, why don't you take them to those two lonely patients of mine in the hospital? Just say 'Hello' to them and see what you can do for them."

Somewhat reluctantly, the woman did as her doctor suggested. By that simple little act, the logjam in her heart was broken. It washed away the bitterness. More and more often she took the flowers to the hospital instead of the cemetery. She found that the healing power of God, which she had been resisting, had finally broken through, and she was freed from the destructive grief that had been diminishing her life. She had moved into the *gracious circle*— and all because of a simple act of mercy.

The more you love, the more you are loved; the more you are loved, the more you are given strength to love.

# A Layer of Silver

An enormously rich man complained to his psychiatrist that despite his great wealth which enabled him to possess everything money could buy, he felt miserable. The doctor took the wealthy man by the hand and escorted him to a window overlooking the street.

"What do you see?" asked the psychiatrist.

"I see men, women and children," the man answered.

Then the psychiatrist escorted the man to a mirror. "Now what do you see?" he asked.

"I see only myself," the man replied.

Then the psychiatrist said, "In the window there is glass and in the mirror there is glass. When you look through the glass in the window you can see others. But behind the glass in the mirror is a layer of silver. When silver is added you cease to see others, you see only yourself."

# PEACE IN THIS WORLD

During World War II, an American warship in the Pacific was transporting some wounded Japanese prisoners. The medical officer in charge took such excellent care of the prisoners that his fellow officers protested.

One of them sarcastically remarked, "Why don't you just let them die the way they let our men die?"

The medical officer replied, "I don't play by their rules. The Japanese warlords tell their soldiers that all Americans are beasts. One day, these prisoners will return to their country knowing they had been lied to. They will be able to say that they were treated with compassion by people who cared for them as human beings. I'm going to do my best to replace the hatred in their hearts with the love of God. That's the only way we're going to ever have peace in this world."

# "I Also See the Good"

A remarkable demonstration of the healing power of God's love was the subject of this report in the *Los Angeles Times*:

She calls herself a "prisoner of love"; inmates call her "The White Angel." Sister Antonia Brenner lives in La Mesa Penitentiary in Tijuana, Mexico—voluntarily—in order to minister to the prisoners. She eats the food inmates eat. She sleeps in a cell. And she answers the call of the guard each morning, just as they do. Sister Antonia, a 56-year-old California native, raised several children before taking her vows.

"This is not a job for me," she says. "It is my calling. The prison is my convent."

Each day after roll call, Sister Antonia enters the men's section and walks about unescorted. She is besieged with requests. If a prisoner's mother is sick, Sister Antonia will visit. If a relative has died, she will go to the funeral. When prisoners need a lawyer, medicine or just a toothbrush, they ask Sister Antonia. Her manner with the more than 1,000 inmates is unique. She deals with forbidding, violent men in a way not usually advised in penology texts. She grabs their cheeks and pinches affectionately; she hugs them, holds their hands. Sister Antonia treats inmates like wayward children who need special attention.

When some suggest she may be naive, Sister Antonia shakes her head. Drawing a dot on a white napkin, she asks, "What do you see? You don't see the white of the napkin. All you see is the dot. With the men here, most outsiders see only that they are murderers or thieves. They don't see the rest of them. I do. Yes, I see the bad in people, but I also see the good."

A young lad always concluded his night prayers with a few supplications. "Dear God," he would say, "please take care of Mommy and Daddy and Baby Brother and Aunt Sara," etc. One night, after the day's events had left him with a troubled heart, he said, "Dear God, please take good care of Mommy, Daddy, Baby Brother, Grandma, Grandpa, Aunt Sara—and please take extra good care of Yourself, or we're all sunk!"

# "YOU HAVE MADE MY LIFE"

A woman attended a meeting at which her former high school music teacher was present. The two began to talk about the distant past and their teacher/student relationship.

"I have always remembered fondly that you gave me much extra time and encouragement. I was so inspired by you that I decided to continue my music education in college and graduate school. Now I am a college professor and the head of the entire music department."

Later, as they said their goodbyes, the teacher said, "Thank you for saying all those nice things about my teaching. You have made my day."

The woman replied, "Oh no, let me thank you. You have made my life!"

# OPPORTUNITIES TO CARE

A school superintendent and an elementary school principal were conducting a review of an eighth grade teacher's work. As they entered the classroom through the back door, they heard the teacher say to the tallest boy in the class, "Leonard, would you please raise the window?" When Leonard raised the window, the teacher said in a voice all could hear, "I don't know what I would do without Leonard. He is the only one who can raise that window for me."

After they had left the classroom, the principal said to the superintendent, "I hope you noticed what a beautiful and sensitive thing that teacher did for the boy named Leonard. Leonard is large for his age—and very awkward. He is slow to learn and desperately needs encouragement. You see, the window really didn't need raising. But Leonard needed to raise the window. He needed recognition. And the teacher, bless her, was responding to this need."

A very simple act, a small act of kindness, yet very important to all of us, because before this week is over we will have dozens of similar opportunities to be sensitive to another's need; opportunities to care!

# Not "Me First"

In the late 1950s, writer Norman Cousins traveled to Lambarene, in the heart of equatorial Africa, to visit Dr. Albert Schweitzer. Schweitzer was a man of many talents and achievements who renounced everything and went into the jungle to minister to the sick.

In the opening pages of his book on Schweitzer, Cousins describes the daily after-dinner ritual of this modern man of humility whom history will forever exalt. When dinner ended, Dr. Schweitzer would announce a hymn to be sung. Then he would position himself at an old upright piano standing against the wall. Norman Cousins writes:

"I doubt whether I shall ever forget my shock and disbelief when, the first evening of my visit, I saw him approach the upright. Earlier in the day, while exploring the hospital on my own, I had wandered into the dining room where Dr. Schweitzer and his staff of fifteen eat each day. The first thing that caught my eye was the piano. It must have been at least 50 years old. The keyboard was badly stained. Large double screws fastened the ivory to each note. I tried to play but drew back almost instantly. The volume pedal was stuck and reverberations of the harsh sounds hung in the air. One or more strings were missing on at least a dozen keys.

"Before coming to Lambarene, I had heard that under equatorial conditions of extreme heat and moisture, one doesn't even try to keep a piano in tune; you make your peace with the inevitable and do the best you can. Even so, when Schweitzer sat down at the piano and propped up the hymn book, I winced. Here was one of history's greatest interpreters of Bach, a man who could fill any concert hall in the world, but he was now about to play a dilapidated upright virtually beyond repair. And he went at it easily and with the dignity that never leaves him."

Here is a medical doctor who once was a distinguished organist and pianist and a leading authority on Johann Sebastian Bach; a man with a record of excellence in philosophy, theology, and history, and a brilliant record as teacher and author. Here was a man with the world at his feet who gave it all up, humbled himself in the truest sense of the word by becoming a servant to the sick in a remote, disease-infested little spot in the African bush.

Again, in Norman Cousins' words, "I felt not only a ping but a certain inspiration in the image of Schweitzer at the old piano. For the amazing and wondrous thing was that the piano seemed to lose its poverty in his hands. The tinniest and chattering echoes seemed subdued, and his being at the piano strangely seemed to make it right. The fact of Schweitzer's being there—his presence— seemed to make everything right, even the primitive and inadequate hospital facilities."

At Lambarene, Schweitzer, received a letter from a professor in France who told him about an examination paper that had been turned in by a nineteen-year-old student. The question that had been asked was, "How would you define the last hope for the culture of Western Europe?" The student had answered, "It is not in any part of Europe. It is in a small African village, and it can be identified with an 82-year-old man."

Dr. Schweitzer said, "In the morning when the sun is up and I hear the cries of the hospital, I do not think of these lofty ideas. But when the hospital is asleep, it means much to me that the student should believe these things. Instead of trying to get acceptance for my ideas, I decided I would make my life my argument. I would advocate the things I believed in terms of the life I lived and what I did. Instead of vocalizing my belief in the existence of God within each of us, I would attempt to have my life and work say what I believed."

PART THREE

# Spinach to Help You See God

## IS GOD IN NEW YORK CITY?

A wealthy woman in New York City died and left a will in which she gave her entire estate to God. This created legal problems which the authorities said could only be resolved in the courts. Consequently, a lawsuit was started in which "God" was named as a party. A summons was issued and the process servers went through the motions of trying to serve it.

The final report sent to the Court read as follows: "After a due and diligent search, made in accordance with established procedures, God cannot be found in New York City."

In the matter of where God can be found, the search does not begin in New York City or any other city. The search begins in our hearts! Are you experiencing God's Presence within you? That is the question!

# WALK RIGHT IN

In his book, *The Nature of the Physical World,* Doctor Arthur Eddington describes the "complicated business" of stepping into a room. He says that as you enter, you must shove against an atmospheric pressure of 14 pounds on every square inch of your body.

Then, having crossed the threshold you must position your foot to land on a surface which is travelling around the sun at the rate of 20 miles per second. And you do all this while hanging from a spinning planet with your head pointed outward into space.

It's all very interesting, especially to the scientists, whose business it is to analyze a common ordinary thing like stepping into a room. The great majority of us simply walk right in.

That's the way it is with belief in God. Long before we begin to analyze, long before we begin to speculate, long before we begin to look for reasons, we simply walk right in. That is to say, we simply believe.

# IN THE BEGINNING

Said the psychiatrist to the patient, "I'm not aware of your problem, so perhaps you should start at the beginning."

Said the patient to the psychiatrist, "All right. In the beginning I created the heavens and the earth..."

That patient's problem is our problem too. It is the big stumbling block we encounter as we move through nothingness toward the light. It is the temptation to try to go it alone. It is the misguided notion that we can get through to the light independently, without God. It is the temptation to rely on our own meager resources for answers to the question of the "why?" of life. It is the temptation to make little gods of ourselves.

One must say to oneself, "All right, in the beginning I did not create the heavens and the earth. That is God's creation. God is the Source of my life. I need God to tell me *who* I am, and *why* I am, and *where* I am going. I need God to lead me through the exit from nothingness into the light of His grand design. I need God to tell me where my fulfillment lies. In the beginning, God created the heavens and the earth."

# A Life-transforming Experience

A woman had been going through a particularly trying period in her life. Instead of turning to God, as many of us do when real problems come, she simply made herself busier, burying herself in her work and other activities. In the midst of this, she was seriously injured in an accident and was hospitalized. While confined to bed, she had time to reflect on what had been happening in her life. She had time to pay attention, to close off everything else and just listen. It became for her a life-transforming experience, a new awareness of God's Presence. In her own words:

"The feeling I had in this moment was a sense of freedom, of being unencumbered. It was as though the windows of my life had been washed. It seemed like some part of me had been left behind—a part that was old and hard. In that hospital bed, the world was a very private world, and I was quite alone. Then, all at once, I was not alone. There was no increase in light; there was no sound, no motion. Lying utterly still, I was aware of a Presence, and I simply waited. Previously unable to accept, I was now accepting. I was allowing myself to be claimed. I was allowing this Grace to watch over me. And I knew what this Presence was. It was the Love of God! Here was the glory of His patient Presence. Feelings of wonder gripped my soul and, with the wonder, peace. Not the peace the world knows, but at-one-ness with God. And I understood. I understood that I was not alone! The Lord was already there!"

A small European village was visited by an earthquake, severe enough to make everything in the town tremble, including the people. The only exception was one of the village matriarchs who remained cool and calm, refusing to come apart and panic as the others did. When it was all over, the old woman was asked how she managed to remain so together, so serene during the crisis. She said, "I just kept on giving thanks for a God who can shake the world."

# Our Crazy Mixed-up Family

If you should ever want to calculate how many ancestors you have had (say, in the past 500 years), start off with your two parents. Each of them had two parents, so multiply two times two. And each of them had two parents, so multiply that number times two. Then continue: two times two times two—21 times. That's 21 generations, and that takes you back 500-600 years. Your final calculation will tell you that over two million ancestors have been swimming in your gene pool.

Each one of us has had millions of unknown characters dancing in our DNA, waltzing with our chromosomes, fiddling with our genetic makeup. Out of those two million or more characters, you can be sure there are some Einsteins and some "asinines," some geniuses and some goofballs, some poets and some "chowder-heads," some lovers and some loners, some paragons of virtue and some demons of degradation—and they are all kinfolk. They may not be "kissin' kin," but they are part of our ancestry—our crazy, mixed-up family, if you will.

Confronting this reality can have a rather humbling effect on us. But running through this mixture of humanity and leading straight to us is a common thread. Each of our ancestors, in her or his own way, thought of God. Each, in her or his own way, sought God, prayed to God, struggled mightily to know God, or desperately tried to ignore God.

God is the vine that runs through our ancestry, continues through us, and on into the future. God is the living breath, the very stuff of our souls. And whether or not our ancestors listened to God's voice, God was still there—with them. And God is still here—with us.

# ALL THE WAY TO HEAVEN

"Some of these mornings, bright and fair, I'm gonna lay down this heavy load," says the lyric in the famous old spiritual entitled, "By and By." Who doesn't feel this way from time to time? This poignant song captures the almost universal longing for a blessed afterlife.

It brings to mind the pious monk of the Middle Ages who observed that many of his fellow Christians were obsessed with worry about the afterlife. Realizing how much of life's goodness they were missing along the way, he authored this beautiful line: "All the way to heaven is heaven."

However we define heaven, one definition stands supreme: to be in perfect union with God. If there is a fence around your heart shutting heaven out until you're dead, move it over! Not only in the sweet "by-and-by," but all the way to heaven is heaven.

Wherever you are, or whatever you're doing right now, God is with you in this present moment. He longs to give you fresh hope. Reach out for heaven now!

## SWAY WITH GOD

The following appeared in the *New York Times* on November 24, 1931:

"The year was 1881. A man was to walk a wire across Niagara Falls with another on his shoulders. After weeks of preliminary practice, the moment for the event arrived. The rope-walker cautioned his young colleague: 'We are about to risk our lives. I am to walk the wire. The whole responsibility is mine. You have nothing to do but match my movements. If I sway to the left, let yourself sway with me. If I sway to the right, do the same. Under no circumstances try to save yourself, for there must be only one will in this adventure, and that will is mine. You must subordinate yours to ensure harmony. There is only one thing for you to do: sway with me.'

"As they drew near the opposite side, the unexpected happened. The long vibration of the wire broke in the center into two waves, and each of these broke again into two, and so on, in accordance with the laws of vibration. And the shortened wavelike movements became so violent that the man could scarcely keep his feet where he placed them. It was a perilous moment, but the feat was accomplished, and the spectacular escapade was a success.

"After this event, the young man who had played the secondary role settled down, married, became a church leader and a solid citizen. And he grew fond of saying, 'I learned more religion on that wire that day than in all my life. I learned that the only safe and sane way to live is to sway with God.'"

For us to "sway" with God we must eat our spiritual spinach. We must choose to subordinate our wills to God's will.

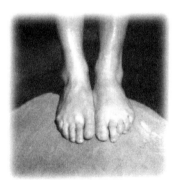

# ALL THERE IS OF YOU

The father of two daughters had just awakened in the morning. His wife was in the kitchen making breakfast. She turned to their two daughters and said, "Run upstairs and tell daddy that breakfast is ready."

They both ran upstairs, but the older one outran her sister and was the first to reach him as he sat on the edge of the bed straightening his tie. She jumped on his knee, put her arms around his neck and kissed him, saying, "Daddy, breakfast is ready."

Then her little sister arrived, puffing and panting and looking a bit crestfallen as she took in the situation. "I've got all there is of Daddy," the big sister taunted. Whereupon, Daddy looked lovingly at the younger daughter and held out his free arm and wrapped it around her and hugged her.

The little sister then looked up at her and said, "You may have all there is of Daddy, but Daddy's got all there is of me!"

The good God who made you, wants you for His own. When you treasure Him in your deepest heart, He's got all there is of you!

# In God's Hands

According to a study made at an agricultural school in Iowa some years ago, the production of 100 baskets of corn from one acre of land required four million pounds of water. It also required 6800 pounds of oxygen, 5200 pounds of carbon, 160 pounds of nitrogen, 125 pounds of potassium, 75 pounds of yellow sulphur, and quantities of other elements too numerous to mention.

In addition to these ingredients, sunshine is required, as well as many hours of the farmer's labor. However, it was estimated that a mere five per cent of the produce of a farm can be attributed to human effort. The rest is in God's hands—and that is something worth remembering when you ponder your ultimate goal in life.

# SWIFT THINGS

A third-grade teacher in a parochial school in Milwaukee published a children's book entitled, "The Littlest Brother." Her pupils had watched the manuscript grow from actual stories told in class. They became so fascinated with the project that they began writing little stories of their own. One child's effort resulted in a work that might have qualified as the shortest book ever written. It consisted of a single sheet of paper, folded down into four pages. On the first page was the title: "Swift Things." On the inside was a lively sketch of a deer. Beneath the deer were these words: "A deer is very swift, but God was already there."

Wherever you have gone in your life, God was already there. Wherever you are going in your life, however swift the journey, God is already there.

# RECEIVING A REVELATION

Once there was a man in desperate need of a revelation from God, for he was gravely ill and in great pain. He had prayed for healing, but the healing did not come. The man thought, *I have served God as well as I have been able. I have failed Him, no doubt—perhaps in large ways, certainly in small ways—but I have served Him. Why does He not help me?*

His wife always helped him. He had merely to voice a request, and she ran to meet it. She even tried to foresee his needs and meet them before he asked. The distressed man saw the look of deep concern in his wife's eyes. He also had a friend who helped him. The friend did his chores, sat by his bed, and comforted him. He saw the same look of deep concern in his friend's eyes.

He found himself saying, almost in astonishment, "These people love me!" Still, no miracle of healing happened when he prayed, and no voice answered when he called, "God, God!" So he continued to cry out in bitterness and doubt.

Then this thought came to the man: "What do I mean when I say 'God'?" It occurred to him that he might be asking for something to happen that he did not even believe in. At times when he cried "God!" he was looking not for God, but for a mighty magician. Yet he did not believe in a mighty magician. At other times he was looking for a kindly old man, like the Lord God Jehovah in "Green Pastures."

Then the man asked himself, *What do I believe about God?* There was one thing he could say with certainty: "God is Love." Suddenly he realized that all the time he had been crying and complaining, the God who is Love had been revealing Himself. The God of Love had been showing Himself through the only faces the man's eyes could see—the faces of his wife and his friend. The God of Love had been speaking through the only voices the man's ears could hear—the voices of his wife and his friend. Then the man realized that all the time he had been begging for a revelation and a miracle, he had been receiving a revelation and a miracle. The name of the revelation and the name of the miracle is Love.

# GOD IS WHAT LIFE IS

When Russian Novelist Leo Tolstoy was about 50 years old, he went into a period of suicidal depression. If you have done any serious reading on suicide, you know that every suicidal person is filled with ambiguity: he wants desperately to destroy himself, but he also wants to live.

One day, in the midst of Tolstoy's depression, he went out walking in the woods. He said that he began to think about God, and he suddenly realized that when he thought "God" he experienced a surge of renewed courage and hope. But he dismissed the thought, and the depression poured in on him again. He repeated this process several times. Later he described the experience in his journal. He said:

> Why do I look further? He is there, He without whom one cannot live. To acknowledge God and to live are the same thing. God is what life is. Well then, live! Seek God! There will be no life without Him!

Tolstoy did not say, naively, that all of his problems were suddenly solved. He did say that he had found the Key.

# PART FOUR

# They Ate Their Spinach!

## THE CAUSE OF ALL YOUR TROUBLE

At a preacher's conference, a hospital chaplain told the story of one of the patients he had been visiting almost daily for several weeks. The patient was college-educated, had a wife and children and a reasonably successful business. Then one day he began to experience stomach pains. His doctor sent him to the hospital for tests that revealed a tumor on the spine. The tumor was removed surgically, leaving the man partially paralyzed for a time. A long period of convalescence was indicated.

As the weeks went by, the patient did not progress as well as the doctors had hoped. He was constantly fretting about the financial rut the illness had put him in. He was anxious about his business. He worried about the future. He was forever asking, "Why did this happen to me?"

One day, as his wife and children stood around his bedside trying their best to comfort him, his mother came into the room. She walked straight to the bed and, without any preliminaries said, "You have put God out of the center of your life. And that's the cause of all your trouble." Then she turned around and left the room.

Later, the man said to the hospital chaplain, "You know, there isn't anything that anybody could have done that would have meant more to me than that gift from my mother. If my mother had brought me a million dollars it wouldn't have done what those words did for me. At that moment I saw what I had been doing with my life, and I was able to open up and put God back in the center."

The story has no "quick-fix" ending. The man did not immediately recover. The convalescence proceeded slowly, and there was a relapse that was nearly fatal. It was a struggle all the way for that man. But he said, "From that moment on everything was different because God's Power was moving in my life again."

# SURRENDER TO GOD

Doctor Jess Lair, a psychologist, has written a book with the unusual title, *I Don't Know Where I'm Going, But I Sure Ain't Lost.* In one part of the book he tells of a meeting with a man named Vince who had been an alcoholic. At age 45, Vince entered the Alcoholics Anonymous program and became sober. Five years later, he was still sober but his life continued to feel empty.

"There must be a better way of life," he said to the people at AA who had taken him off skid row. "Can you guys tell me what you've got that makes you smile?"

They said to him, "Vince, you cannot have good, long-term, happy sobriety unless you get into the spiritual part of the program."

Commenting on this, Doctor Lair writes:

"I was struck by this gigantic experiment with one million subjects. Here were a million people seized by the most powerful compulsion we find in society today. And here was a system that could stop it! What is it? What makes it work? I started looking at the system as an experimental psychologist, and I came to see that the heart of the system is a deep surrender to God... That's the crucial part of the system, and without that surrender, the system can't get a person sober on a long-term basis. And especially it won't work to give them the happiness and contentment they would like to find in life."[5]

The world-famous social scientist, Aldous Huxley, once spent a semester at Massachusetts Institute of Technology (M.I.T.) as Distinguished Professor in the Humanities. One of Huxley's colleagues managed to engage Huxley in conversation for hours on end, trying to learn all he could from the famous scholar. Later, when asked about his long conversations with Huxley, the colleague said he was most impressed by something he said, almost casually, in a quiet moment: "You know, it's rather embarrassing to have spent one's entire lifetime pondering the human condition and to come toward its close and find that I really don't have anything more profound to pass on by way of advice than, 'Try to be a little kinder.'"

# How Sweet It Is

If you know anything at all about football, you know that there is a fifteen-yard penalty for "unnecessary roughness." In a Bud Blake comic strip called "Tiger," some little boys decide to play a game of football. They divide into two teams only to discover that they need one more player to make the sides even. There are no other boys in sight, so they recruit a little girl, and the game begins. On the first play, the speedy little girl runs for a touchdown. The only little boy that could have stopped her just stood and watched. When criticized by his teammates for not tackling her, he said, "I was afraid I'd hurt her. I guess I should be penalized for unnecessary gentleness..."

Eat your spiritual spinach! Down it daily and, if all goes well, you too may display "unnecessary gentleness" (as do the other spiritual spinach eaters depicted in this section).

# THEY WERE PEOPLE

Enmity transformed into compassion is a theme that runs through the writings of the Russian poet, Yevgeny Yevtushenko. In his autobiography, Yevtushenko tells the story of the day in 1944 when his mother took him from Siberia to Moscow. There they saw some 20,000 German prisoners of war being marched through the streets:

"The pavements swarmed with onlookers, cordoned off by soldiers and police. The crowd was mostly women—Russian women with hands roughened by hard work, lips untouched by lipstick, and with thin hunched shoulders which had borne half the burden of the war. Every one of them must have had a father or husband, a brother or a son killed by the Germans. They gazed with hatred in the direction from which the column was to appear.

"At last we saw it. The generals marched at the head, massive chins stuck out—their whole demeanor meant to show superiority over these common people who had defeated them. The women were clenching their fists. The Russian soldiers and police officers had all they could do to hold them back.

"Then, all at once something happened to

them. They saw ordinary German soldiers— thin, unshaven, wearing dirty, bloodstained bandages, hobbling on crutches or leaning on the shoulders of their comrades, walking with their heads down. The street became dead silent—the only sound was the shuffling of boots and the thumping of crutches.

"Then I saw an elderly woman in broken-down boots push herself forward and touch a police officer's shoulder, saying, 'Let me through.' There must have been something about her that made him step aside. She went up to the column, took from inside her coat something wrapped in a colored handkerchief, and unfolded it. It was a crust of black bread. She pushed it awkwardly into the pocket of a soldier, so exhausted that he was tottering on his feet. And now from every side women were running toward the soldiers, pushing into their hands bread, cigarettes, whatever they had. The soldiers were no longer enemies. They were people."

# "Doctor, When Do I Die?"

There is a beautiful little story that has been handed down in the medical profession. It is about a seven-year-old boy who had an illness which the doctors thought was going to be fatal. He recovered, and then his five-year-old sister contracted the illness. In her case, blood was needed for a transfusion. The blood had to come from a person who had recovered from the disease. The medical people searched everywhere but couldn't find the right person.

As the situation became more critical, they realized that they might have to take blood from the seven-year-old boy—the little girl's brother. Even though they were reluctant to transfuse blood from a child so young, this seemed to be the only way open to save the patient. Consequently, they began to arrange for the procedure. The doctors talked to the little boy, explaining thoroughly what was going to happen, what he was being asked to do.

After thinking it over for several hours, the seven-year-old boy agreed to go through with it. Then came the time when the two children were laying side-by-side, and the transfusion was taking place. The little boy's cheeks were growing pale and the little girl's cheeks were taking on color. The doctors hovered over them because of the delicate situation, but they were pleased because everything was going well.

At this point, the little boy looked up at the doctor nearest him and asked, "Doctor, when do I die?" The doctor suddenly realized that this little boy hadn't understood at all. He thought they had asked him to give his life in order that his sister might live.

This little boy must have had a big helping of spiritual spinach!

# ERNIE'S INVENTION

A college Professor tells the story of how his life was turned around because of a humble man's willingness to risk time and money in his future .

"I spent most of my high school days in the principal's office being disciplined for creating problems in class. My family life was a mess and I worked out my frustration in the classroom. I gained a reputation as a trouble-maker.

"As punishment for some of my anti-social behavior, I was given work detail after school. The school janitor, Ernie, was a short, stocky man who spoke English with a heavy accent. He worked quickly and demanded that I do the same—all the time peppering me with questions about my interests and ambitions. At the end of my forced work, Ernie asked me if I was interested in a part-time job. I couldn't believe anyone was willing to hire me, but quickly said yes.

"Under Ernie's direction, I worked after school every day for two hours. He talked to me as a friend and complimented each task I completed. Gradually I began to like myself better and trips to the discipline office grew less frequent. I graduated at 18 and enlisted in the service. Ernie came down to the bus station to give me my final pay, and a bear hug for good luck.

"I loved Ernie, but it wasn't until many years later that I learned just how special he really was. My part-time job had been Ernie's invention and my pay had not come from funds budgeted by the School Board but out of his own meager earnings. The stocky man with the big heart paid to save a troubled kid—and it worked."

God's will is for you to experience His loving Presence in every life situation. He has given you a mission to perform; a work to be done; a goal to be achieved; a victory to be won. God's will is for you to express His loving Presence in the grime and sweat of the human arena; in the give-and-take, rough-and-tumble real world; in the joys and the sorrows; in both the easy relationships and the difficult ones.

# SORE FINGER

In the 1920s, a group of men met in the home of Dwight Morrow, a close friend and admirer of Calvin Coolidge. The meeting's purpose was to evaluate Coolidge and some others as potential candidates for the office of President of the United States. The discussion finally centered on Coolidge. Some thought he would make a good candidate. Others disagreed, saying that he wasn't colorful enough. One of the participants then summed up the group's consensus, saying, "The people just wouldn't like him."

Whereupon, Dwight Morrow's six-year-old daughter, who had quietly slipped into the room, made her presence known. She held out one hand and pointed to a finger on the other which had a band-aid taped around it. Then she said, "When we all were sitting at the table having lunch, Mr. Coolidge was the only one who asked me about my sore finger."

# SHARED SECRET

Sir William Osler is among the most highly esteemed physicians in modern medical history. The classic two-volume biography of Osler abounds with stories depicting not only his genius as a practitioner of medicine, but also his unusually compassionate nature.

It is said that one day he entered the pediatric ward of a London hospital and noted with delight the children who were playing at one end of the room. Then his gaze was drawn to one small girl who sat off to one side alone on her bed, a doll in her arms. She was clearly oppressed by feelings of loneliness.

A question about her to the head nurse brought the response that she was ostracized by the other children. Her mother was dead, Osler was told; her father had paid but one visit, bringing at that time the doll, which she now tightly clutched. Apart from that one visit, no one had ever come to see her again. As a result, the other children, concluding that she was unimportant, had treated her with disdain.

Sir William was at his best in moments like that, and he immediately walked to the child's bed. "May I sit down, please?" he asked in a voice loud enough to carry to where the other children were at play. "I can't stay long on this visit, but I have wanted to see you so badly." Those describing the moment say that the girl's eyes became electric with joy.

For several minutes the physician conversed with her in quiet, almost secretive tones. He inquired about her doll's health and appeared to be carefully listening to its heart with his stethoscope. And then as he rose to leave, his voice lifted again so that everyone heard, "You won't forget our secret will you? And mind you, don't tell anyone!" As Osler left the room, he turned to see the once ignored youngster now the center of attention of every other child on the ward.

That wise physician created a safe place with the child for a moment, shared a secret or two, and restored her personal passion for life. His attentiveness and intimacy affirmed her specialness in her own eyes and the eyes of others.

# THIS IS LIVING!

Several years ago, a gifted American surgeon decided to become a medical missionary. He traveled thousands of miles and set up a practice on a Pacific island where the people were suffering greatly for lack of medical assistance.

Some time later, the doctor's former pastor in the U.S. paid him a surprise visit. When the pastor arrived, the doctor was preparing to operate on an eight-year-old girl. The pastor observed through a window in the small hut where the operation took place. Three hours later, the surgeon finally stepped back from the table in the makeshift operating room and said, "She's okay. Going to be all right now." Then he went outside and joined his pastor.

As they talked about what had just taken place, the pastor asked, "How much money would you have received for that operation back home in the States?"

"Oh, thousands of dollars, I suppose," the doctor replied.

"And how much will you receive here?" the pastor asked. "I don't know, just a few cents and the smile of God," said the surgeon. Then he put his hand on the pastor's shoulder, shook it a little, and said, "But man, this is living!"

# "I Really Love This Teacher!"

Nothing seemed to be going right for a certain teacher in a Texas panhandle school. She told it this way...

"Last night I attended an incredibly long PTA meeting. My 30 first-graders seemed to squirm restlessly all day long today. The reading classes were obviously moving backward. At noon, the principal called me into his office. I had forgotten to turn in an important report. The two playground periods were hot, windy, and gritty with dust. The final straw fell when I snagged my last good stockings just after the bell rang. At that precise moment, Mrs. Jones burst into the classroom weeping because her Mary was no longer in the top reading group. I yearned to go home to a relaxing tub, but today there was a special meeting scheduled at which a distinguished educator was to speak. She talked about the new era that was coming in education. To be prepared for it she said we must always be professional-minded. The longer she talked, the less professional I felt. She seemed to know all my secret sins as a teacher."

The school teacher's lament doesn't end there. Later, on her weekly 50-mile journey to the university where she was working toward her Master's Degree, an idea struck her which she found irresistible: *I will stop teaching! There is more to life than this and I mean to find it. I'll write a book. I'll grow a garden. But I won't teach school.*

When she arrived, she collapsed into her seat and did not even try to listen to her professor. After all, what was the use? She wouldn't be coming back. But she was wrong.

Again in her own words: "The friendly woman who sat next to me in class leaned over and said, 'I saw an admirer of yours the other day.'

"I sat up straight and asked, 'Really?' I listened with growing interest as she continued.

"'I was in the bus station last week, waiting for my son, when I noticed a Mexican woman and her little girl. The mother didn't speak English, but I talked with the little girl. She told me that she and her mother were on their way to Colorado to join her father. She said that she was now in the second grade, and she told me her teacher's name. Then she reached into her pocket and pulled out a photograph. 'I really love this teacher,' she said. I was astonished to see that it was your picture—faded, ragged, and almost worn out. When I said I knew you, the little girl told her mother. They both beamed with joy and acted as if they wanted to kiss me." My friend paused, waiting for my reply. I was trying to remember the little Latin Americans in last year's class. Finally I asked, "Was the little girl's name Julia?" It wasn't. "Then was it Adelina?" It was Adelina.

The school teacher went home that night and did some deep thinking and some heavy praying about that conversation, and about herself. She pictured little Adelina pointing to her photograph and saying, "I really love this teacher." Then, she renewed her decision to change—not her profession—but her attitude.

"The thought of Adelina's small face as she innocently showed my picture to a stranger in a bus station will never cease to warm my heart," she said. "Stop school teaching? Why, what would I do?"

# Permission to Cross the Street

A middle-aged woman named Harriet was trying to decide what to do with the rest of her life. To help her decide, she took a job in a hospital chaplain's office.

One day, when the chaplain was not at the hospital, a distraught, tired-looking man came into the office and said, "I'm not sure what I'm looking for but my father seems to need to talk to someone before he can die. We're not church people, but I decided to come here anyway. Something is holding my dad back. He can't seem to let go. Your name tag says 'Chaplain,' so would you please come and see what you can do?"

Harriet began to panic. She was not a chaplain. She was not even a social worker. But this man needed help. So she followed him into a darkened room where a pale, emaciated old man lay on the bed. She touched his shoulder gently. He acknowledged her presence with a flutter of his eyelids. She asked if he wanted to pray with her. Again, a flutter of the eyelids. In her anxious state, the only prayer she could think of was the one she taught to her children when they were little ones: "Now I lay me down to sleep/I pray the Lord my soul to keep." Again, she touched the man's shoulder to put him at ease, but still something was wrong. Then Harriet remembered her final gesture in those long-ago experiences of putting her kids to bed. "I can do that," she said to herself, "mothers do that." And she gave the dying man a gentle kiss, and left the room.

Later, the son sought her out. "Thank you," he said. "I don't know what you did, but right after you left the room, he peacefully drifted away." Without thinking, Harriet replied, "Oh, I gave him permission to cross the street."

# Our Lady of the Daily Mail

Healing is an important subject for us, not only because we want to be healthy, but because God has called us to be instruments of healing to others.

Irene R. Deuel, health-care professional, tells this lovely story about the healing ministry of a woman named Sue Reed, to whom she gave the title, "Our Lady of the Daily Mail":

"While working as a nurse, I took care of an eight year old crippled boy. One day he asked me to read him a letter from his 'Aunt Sue.' The letter ran more like a diary:

> Dear Frankie,
> Today you and I will take the bugs off
> the potato vines. Get a stick and can,
> hold the can under the bug and knock
> it off with the stick. When the can is
> full, I'll show you what to do.

"The letter went on with another chore for Frankie, talked about a collie named 'Brother,' gave all the details of a picnic, and ended with a beautiful story about an elf who painted butterfly wings.

"Frankie had never seen his 'Aunt Sue,'

but he lived for those letters. He was confined to a wheelchair, but through them he led the life of a healthy, active farm boy, jumping fences, tearing his britches, climbing apple trees, and running through the fields with "Brother" at his heels.

"One day he was near the village where Aunt Sue mailed her letters, and stopped to ask the postmaster if he knew her.

"'A Miss Sue Reed mails letters every day to children in hospitals,' he said. 'There she comes now.' I looked in the direction he pointed and saw a lady in a wheelchair making her way slowly toward us. 'Miss Reed's been crippled since she was 12,' said the Postmaster. 'All she does is sit and write. What I can't figure out is how she'd have anything to write about.'"

# AN EMPTY SACK

Three men set out on a journey. Each carried two sacks around his neck—one in front and one in back.

The first man was asked what was in his sacks. "In this one on my back," he said, "I carry all the kind deeds of my friends. In that way, they are out of sight and I don't have to think about them. This sack in front carries all the unkind things people do to me. I pause in my journey everyday to take them out, lest I forget them. It slows me down, but nobody gets away with anything."

The second man said, "In this one on my back, I keep all my bad deeds. I keep them behind me, out of my view. This sack in front carries my good deeds. I constantly keep them before me. I pause in my journey every day to take them out, lest I forget them. It slows me down, but I take great pleasure in them."

The third man said, "I carry my friends' kind deeds in this front sack," he said. "It looks full, but it is not heavy. Far from slowing me down, it is like the sails of a ship. It helps me move ahead. The sack on my back has a hole in the bottom. That's where I put all the evil I hear from others. It just falls out and is lost, so I have no burden to impede me."

Guess who finished first!

# A Word Of Hope

Many years ago, on the busiest block of Main Street in a small midwestern town, a smooth cement sidewalk was laid to replace the old, rough brick path. The newly laid cement was covered for several days while it dried out. A little civic ceremony was arranged to celebrate the uncovering, and most of the townspeople turned out for the event.

The mayor stepped up to do the honors and, as he rolled up the covering to expose the new sidewalk, a strange silence came over the crowd. Then, suddenly, it seemed that everyone was either smiling tenderly or had tears rolling down their cheeks. For there on the new sidewalk, for the length of the entire block, the tiny footprints of a barefoot toddling baby were embedded in the cement.

Today, those footprints are still there. And anyone in town will tell you that heavy hearts have never passed down that street without being cheered by the sight of those baby footprints and without deriving some degree of hope from the sight of those baby footprints. They're a poignant reminder of their Source, the tenderhearted God of love.

# Afterword

I hope that this book will contribute in some
way to the enrichment of your life
and help you to treasure it
as a priceless gift from God.

# ENDNOTES

1   J.D. Freeman, *Love Speaks* (Unity Village, MO:
    Unity, 1980, adapted)

2   D. Spatz. and A. Bodine, *Look At It This Way*
    (Baltimore: Bodine & Assoc., 1975)

3   *Which One's Cliff?* (London: Hodder &
    Stoughton, 1977)

4   Helen Hayes, *My Life in Three Acts* (New York:
    Simon and Schuster, Inc., 1981)

5.  Dr. Jess Lair, *I Don't Know Where I'm Going,
    But I Sure Ain't Lost* (New York: Ballantine
    Books,  1983)

For more information about *Spiritual Spinach* resources, please visit us on the web at:

http://www.spiritualspinach.com
E-mail: author@spiritualspinach.com

Or write:

Spiritual Spinach
James F. Colaianni
P.O. Box 3102
Margate, NJ  08402